THIS WALKER BOOK BELONGS TO:

_____

_____

_____

_____

In the CITY

Illustrated by
Sally Hobson

WALKER BOOKS
AND SUBSIDIARIES
LONDON · BOSTON · SYDNEY

broom
broom

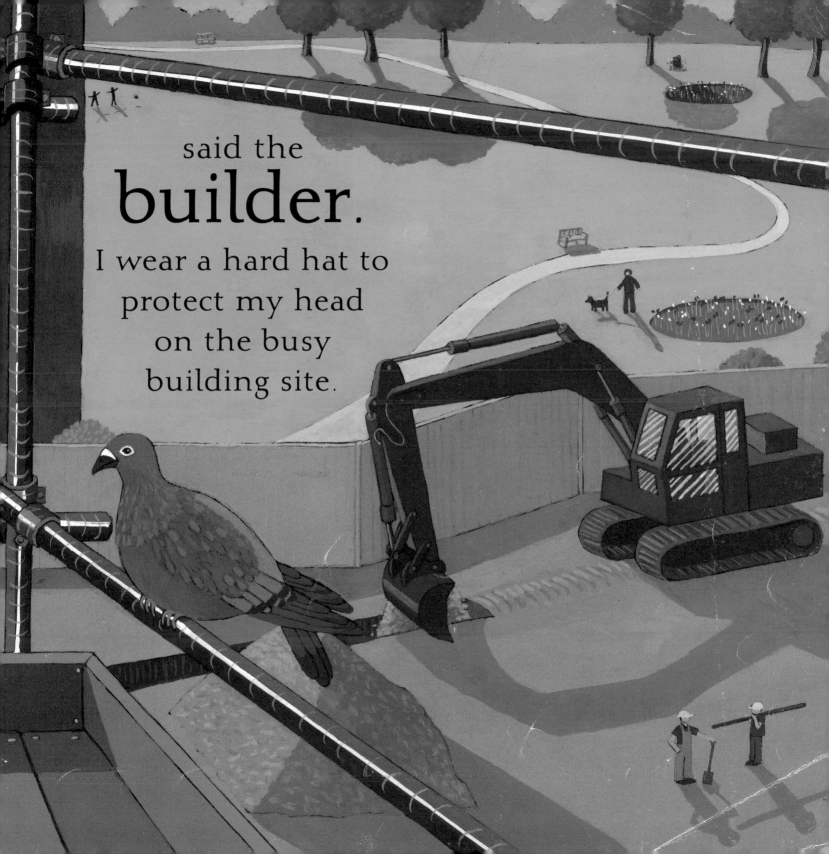

said the **builder.**

I wear a hard hat to protect my head on the busy building site.

Mine!

said the
pigeon.

At night I perch on
rooftops and window
ledges and go to sleep.

said the
sales assistant.
I work in a very large shop
called a department store.

dig
dig

said the
gardener.

I plant flowers in all
the parks and look
after them.

Here we are, in the city.
Can you find the builder, the pigeon,
the gardener, the cat, the bus driver
and the sales assistant?

First published 2001 by Walker Books Ltd
87 Vauxhall Walk, London SE11 5HJ

This edition published 2002

2 4 6 8 10 9 7 5 3 1

Series concept by Louise Jackson

Words by Paul Harrison and Louise Jackson

Designed by Justin Hunt

Wildlife consultant: Martin Jenkins

Text © 2001 Walker Books Ltd
Illustrations © 2001 Sally Hobson

This book has been typeset in Calligraphic

Printed in Hong Kong

British Library Cataloguing in Publication Data:
a catalogue record for this book is available
from the British Library

ISBN 0-7445-7750-0

Walker Flip-flap Facts

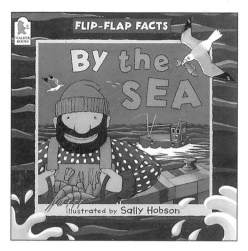

ISBN 0-7445-7748-9 (pb)

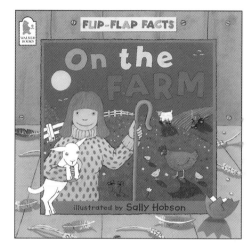

ISBN 0-7445-7749-7 (pb)

ISBN 0-7445-7750-0 (pb)

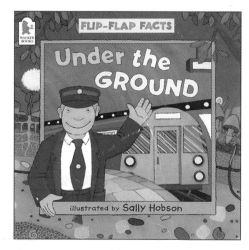

ISBN 0-7445-7751-9 (pb)

Collect them all!